A GRAPHIC HISTORY OF THE AMERICAN WEST

THE GOLD RUSH

BY GARY JEFFREY
ILLUSTRATED BY EMANUELE BOCCANFUSO

Gareth Stevens
Publishing

Please visit our website, www.garethstevens.com.
For a free color catalog of all our high-quality books,
call toll free 1-800-542-2595 or fax 1-877-542-2596.

Library of Congress Cataloging-in-Publication Data

Jeffrey, Gary.
The Gold Rush / Gary Jeffrey.
p. cm. — (A graphic history of the American West)
Includes index.
ISBN 978-1-4339-6741-2 (pbk.)
ISBN 978-1-4339-6742-9 (6-pack)
ISBN 978-1-4339-6739-9 (library binding)
1. California—Gold discoveries—Juvenile literature. 2. Voyages to the
Pacific Coast—Juvenile literature. 3. Overland journeys to the Pacific—
Juvenile literature. I. Title.
F865.J44 2012
979.4'04—dc23
2011022834

First Edition

Published in 2012 by
Gareth Stevens Publishing
111 East 14th Street, Suite 349
New York, NY 10003

Printed in China

CPSIA compliance information: Batch #DW12GS: For further information contact Gareth Stevens, New York, New York at 1-800-542-2595.

CONTENTS

FREE FOR ALL

The territory of California originally belonged to Spain and then Mexico. In 1846, the United States went to war with Mexico over a border dispute about Texas. Their victory in 1848 secured not only Texas but many new lands, including California.

Sutter's Mill on the American River, Coloma.

AN AMAZING DISCOVERY

Swiss emigrant John Sutter came to California in 1847 and built a fort near present-day Sacramento. He then asked a carpenter, James Marshall, to build a sawmill in the Sierra Nevada foothills. Marshall had just finished the mill in January 1848 when he spotted flakes of pure gold in the water.

Sutter tried to keep the discovery a secret, but soon employees were leaving his fort (below) in droves to look for gold in the hills. His sawmill also got abandoned.

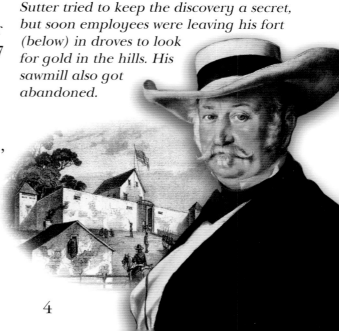

During 1848, gold could be easily panned in the river or chipped out of rocks.

RICH PICKINGS

At first, people in the quiet port of San Francisco disbelieved the stories. It took storekeeper Sam Brennan parading through the streets with a bottle of gold chips to start the rush. Briefly the town emptied as all its men took off—a pattern that would be repeated on a grand scale.

In December 1848, President Polk told the world about California gold.

GOLD FEVER!

In the New Year, fortune hunters flocked to San Francisco from every corner of the globe. In the eastern states, even sober and sensible men seemed powerless to resist. Journeys west were organized by ship or overland trail. The trail, crossing mountains and deserts, was especially hazardous, but the lure of gold was too strong…

An 1849 handbill advertising passage to California and (below) a map of the goldfields

FOR
CALIFORNIA!
DIRECT
EXTRAORDINARY INDUCEMENTS!!
THIRTY-FIVE DAYS TO THE GOLD REGIONS!
The "California Steam Navigation Co."
Will dispatch their first vessel from New York, the NEW and SPLENDID
STEAM SHIP!
NICARAGUA

On **FRIDAY, MARCH 23d**

200 JACK ASS

The Quickest, Safest and
Price of Passage Through

MAP OF THE GOLD REGIONS OF CALIFORNIA.
Showing the Routes via Chagres and Panama, Cape Horn, &c.

IMPORTANT DIRECTIONS

DESCRIPTION OF CALIFORNIA

5

William Swain—Forty-Niner

IN YOUNGSTOWN, NEW YORK, APRIL 1849, WILLIAM SWAIN'S OLDER BROTHER, GEORGE, HELPED HIM LUG HIS TRUNK TO THE BUGGY.

IF THE PICKINGS ARE AS RICH AS THEY SAY, WILLIAM, I WILL FOLLOW YOU OUT NEXT SPRING!

GOLD FEVER TAKES HOLD IN CALIFORNIA

MRS. SWAIN WASN'T HAPPY...

OH WILLIAM, YOU MIGHT AS WELL BE GOING TO THE **ENDS OF THE EARTH!**

HUSH, SABRINA. AS SOON AS I MAKE TEN THOUSAND I'LL BE BACK, *I PROMISE*.

TWENTY-SEVEN-YEAR-OLD SWAIN LEFT BEHIND HIS STEADY, IF UNEXCITING, LIFE AS A FRUIT FARMER FOR THE OVERLAND TRAIL TO CALIFORNIA, DETERMINED TO...

...CLAIM MY **DESTINY**.

YA!.

IN MISSOURI, HE PAID $100 TO JOIN A STOCK COMPANY CALLED THE "WOLVERINE RANGERS." ON THE GREAT PLAINS, THEIR OX-DRAWN TEAMS JOINED HUNDREDS OF OTHER GOLD SEEKERS HEADED **WEST.**

THE LINE OF WAGONS STRETCHED FROM HORIZON TO HORIZON.

THE PLAINS OF NEBRASKA TERRITORY GAVE WAY TO DUSTY SAGEBRUSH DESERT DOTTED WITH POISONED ALKALI LAKES. THE TRAIL WAS LITTERED WITH DEAD ANIMALS LIKE A **BONEYARD**.

AT SOUTH PASS, THEY SHIVERED THEIR WAY ACROSS THE **CONTINENTAL DIVIDE**.

THE SNOWY SIERRA NEVADA WERE THE LAST OBSTACLE ON THE EXHAUSTING TREK. BY MID-NOVEMBER, SWAIN HAD MADE IT TO **CALIFORNIA**.

HE PANNED FOR GOLD UNTIL...

THERE NOW, THAT WAS EASY WORK!

HE WAS PAID IN **GOLD DUST.**

FIFTY DOLLARS!

MERE POCKET MONEY, BUT STILL...

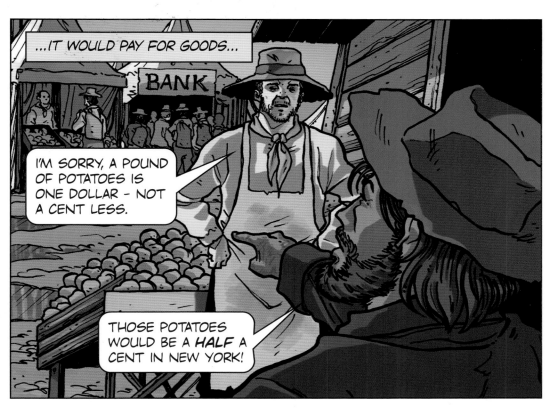

...IT WOULD PAY FOR GOODS...

I'M SORRY, A POUND OF POTATOES IS ONE DOLLAR — NOT A CENT LESS.

THOSE POTATOES WOULD BE A **HALF** A CENT IN NEW YORK!

SUPPLY AND DEMAND. WHEN THE ROADS DRY OUT, THE PRICES WILL COME DOWN.

THE GOLDFIELD WAS AN EXPENSIVE PLACE TO LIVE.

DURING APRIL, SWAIN TREKKED INTO THE MOUNTAINS TO CHECK OUT THE HIGH STREAMS. WHAT HE SAW THERE **ALARMED** HIM.

SO MUCH SNOW, THE RIVER IS ALMOST BURIED!

WHEN SUMMER COMES, THAT'LL MELT AND KEEP THE RIVER AS HIGH AS EVER.

HE HAD BEEN AWAY A YEAR.

BACK DOWN THE VALLEY, SWAIN WENT INTO STRINGTOWN.

HE PASSED BY THE ROUGH TAVERNS...

SEEMS THE ONLY WAY TO MAKE TEN THOUSAND THESE DAYS IS TO WAGER YOUR DUST AT THE CARD TABLE...

BUT SWAIN WASN'T TEMPTED.

DURING JUNE, THEY FINALLY GOT TO MINE THE BEDROCK.

HERE WE GO BOYS - PAY DIRT!

BUT THE RIVERBED WAS BARREN OF GOLD.

WE'RE NOT GOING TO MAKE OUR PILE HERE, BOYS!

YOU DON'T KNOW THAT. TEN YARDS FURTHER ON THE RIVERBED COULD BE *FULL* OF GOLD!

COULD BE. BUT MOST LIKELY WON'T BE.

THAT'S WHY IT'S CALLED THE *CALIFORNIA LOTTERY!*

SWAIN'S HEART *ACHED* TO SEE HIS WIFE AND FAMILY, BUT *PRIDE* WOULDN'T LET HIM QUIT JUST YET.

IN SEPTEMBER, HE TRIED HIS LUCK AT ANOTHER CLAIM, BUT A FREAK STORM WASHED THE DIGGINGS AWAY.

FEVERISH, HE WENT BACK TO THE CABIN ON THE FEATHER.

I THOUGHT CALIFORNIA HAD A LITTLE MORE FOR ME, BUT...

WITH JUST $500 DOLLARS IN GOLD DUST TO HIS NAME, SWAIN CALLED IT QUITS.

SOON SWAIN WAS ON A SOUTHBOUND STEAMER PASSING THROUGH THE GOLDEN GATE.

FAREWELL, EL DORADO!

BACK HOME, HE BECAME A FARMER AGAIN AND HAD THREE MORE CHILDREN WITH SABRINA.

SWAIN HADN'T STRUCK IT RICH, BUT HE'D HAD A GRAND ADVENTURE. HE CLAIMED HIS DESTINY BY BECOMING THE BIGGEST PEACH FARMER IN THE COUNTY OF NIAGARA.

THE END

21

Bottomed Out

Like many forty-niners, Swain got to the party too late. After 1850, the remaining gold could only be got out by machine methods. Corporations took over. Miners worked for a wage as employees, and there was no rush for that.

Miners use water jets to wash the gold out of cliffs at the end of the gold rush.

Rounded Up

About $16 billion worth (in today's money) was dug out over five years. The great inrush of people encouraged calls for statehood, and in 1850, California became the 31st state. Jefferson's dream of a continental America was realized. The gold rush ruined John Sutter when squatters swarmed over his lands. It also changed the American character—never before had people thought to "get rich quick."

The population of San Francisco alone jumped from 1,000 to 25,000 between 1848 and 1849.

GLOSSARY

alkali lakes Lakes that have a higher concentration of natural salts, making the water unsafe for drinking.

barren Without promise, unfruitful, bare.

continental America The land that makes up the United States from the Atlantic Ocean on the east to the Pacific Ocean on the west.

divert To change from a set path.

droves Large crowds of people or animals in motion.

emigrant A person who leaves their home country to settle in another.

fledgling A term for birds just learning to fly, also used to describe something young or inexperienced.

forty-niners The nickname for those who went out to California in 1849 in search of gold.

hazardous Dangerous, risky, unsafe.

sober Quiet, reserved, reasonable.

wager To bet or risk something on the outcome of an activity like a game or competition.

INDEX